Horrid Henry's
Annual 2017

Horrid Henry's
Annual 2017

Francesca Simon

Illustrated by Tony Ross

Orion
Children's Books

ORION CHILDREN'S BOOKS

First published in Great Britain in 2016
by Hodder and Stoughton

1 3 5 7 9 10 8 6 4 2

Compiled by Sally Byford from the Horrid Henry books
by Francesca Simon & illustrated by Tony Ross

A CIP catalogue record for this book
is available from the British Library.

ISBN 978 1 5101 0128 9

Printed and bound in China

The paper and board used in this book are from well-managed forests
and other responsible sources.

FSC
www.fsc.org

MIX
Paper from
responsible sources
FSC® C104740

Orion Children's Books
An imprint of
Hachette Children's Group
Part of Hodder and Stoughton
Carmelite House
50 Victoria Embankment
London EC4Y 0DZ

An Hachette UK Company
www.hachette.co.uk
www.hachettechildrens.co.uk
www.horridhenry.co.uk

Contents

HELLO, FANS!

Too slow racing downstairs to grab the TV remote? Horrible brother or sister plonked in front of the computer even though it's definitely your turn?

Do not fret, oh Purple Hand gang members! Because I, Henry, have raced to your rescue with my brand new rootin'-tootin' action-packed fun galore Annual! There's enough jokes, puzzles and crosswords to keep you busy for ages. To say nothing of all the helpful hints for plots and tricks to play on any evil enemies who have the nerve not to hand over the TV remote when ordered.

Happy Horrid New Year!

Henry

Horrid Henry's New Year Resolutions

Horrid Henry has written lots of good New Year resolutions this year.
But they aren't for himself – they are to hand out to his friends and enemies!

Greedy Graham

I won't eat any sweets this year. Instead, I'll give them all to Henry. He needs them much more than me because his mean parents give him carrot sticks instead of sweets!

Moody Margaret

It's always good to share and my resolution this year is to share all the Secret Club's Triple Choc Chip Marshmallow Chewies with the Purple Hand Gang. Actually, they can have all of them because they are the best club ever!

Rabid Rebecca

This year I'm going to work hard at my homework. Which means I won't have any time to babysit Henry.

12

Mum

I'll do all the chores myself instead of forcing poor hard-working Henry to do them. Peter can still help me though, because he's always so mean to Henry and tries to get him into trouble.

MY NEW YEAR RESOLUTION:
To tame my parents so that they let me do whatever I want! ha ha!

Miss Battle-Axe

I won't give any homework this year, spelling tests are banned, and there'll be no boring Old Town Museum for the school trip – we'll go to the Frosty Freeze Ice Cream Factory instead.

Stuck-Up Steve

My resolution is to stop being such a stuck-up, slimy little toad. The first thing I'm going to do is to give my amazing cousin, Henry, all the brand-new toys I got for Christmas.

Horrid Henry's Parent-Taming Quiz

Here's Horrid Henry's own New Year Resolution; he thinks it will be easy-peasy to tame his pathetic parents. Try Henry's quiz and see if you can spot his top tips and tactics for parent-taming.

1. What's the top tactic to wheedle more pocket money out of your parents?

a. Tell them that everyone else in the whole school gets loads more than you.
b. Shout at them: "YOU'RE THE MEANEST PARENTS IN THE WORLD!"
c. Politely explain that you need more money to buy a nice nature kit.

2. How can you get away with watching loads of TV?

a. Tell your parents it's for homework.
b. Demand they buy a TV for your bedroom.
c. Actually, it isn't sensible to watch too much TV, especially when there's homework to be done.

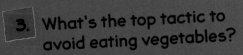

3. What's the top tactic to avoid eating vegetables?

a. Tell your parents you're allergic to all vegetables, especially sprouts.
b. Scream: "I HATE VEGETABLES! BLECCCH!"
c. Politely ask for a very small portion.

4. How can you delay your bedtime?

a. Get ready for bed slowly, and then keep coming downstairs for a drink of water.
b. Have a tantrum.
c. Don't delay your bedtime – children need lots of sleep.

5. What's the top tip for getting out of your chores?

a. Do your chores slowly and badly. In the end, your parents will let you off and do all the housework themselves.
b. Yell at them: "YOU'RE THE LAZIEST PARENTS IN THE WORLD!"
c. Never get out of your chores – your poor parents deserve your help.

6. How can you make your parents feel so guilty that they try hard to be nicer in future?

a. Tell them that all your friends' parents are really fantastic.
b. Yell at them: "YOU'RE THE WORST PARENTS IN THE WORLD!"
c. Tell them that they are the best parents ever … but there are one or two little ways they could be better.

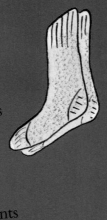

7. What's the best way to tell your parents that socks and underwear are NOT presents?

a. Look sad and tell your parents about all the amazing toys your friends have received.
b. Have a tantrum in Toy Heaven until your parents buy you what you want.
c. Write a neat little wish list and leave it on the table for your parents to find.

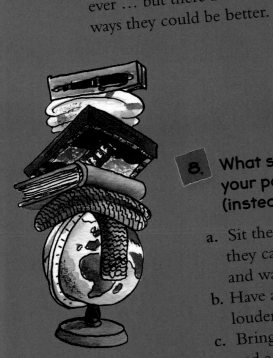

8. What should you do if your parents have a tantrum (instead of you!)?

a. Sit them on the naughty step until they calm down. (Then sneak off and watch TV!)
b. Have a tantrum back – but much louder and longer than theirs!
c. Bring them a nice cup of tea and a biscuit.

Horrid Henry's Secret Stuff

Everyone knows I'm the Lord High Excellent Majesty of the Universe and that I love watching TV, eating crisps and pizza and playing tricks on Peter. But as one of my greatest fans, you deserve to know some extra-special stuff about me.

I'm such a brilliant shot with my Goo-Shooter, I can hit Perfect Peter's nose from 30 paces away.

I do loads of walking. I bet that surprised you! I walk to the TV. I walk to the computer. I walk to the sweet jar and all the way back to the comfy black chair. I don't need to do any more walking!

When I'm King, I'm going to ban Mother's Day. Any parent trying to force their child to celebrate this horrible day will be buried headfirst in quicksand.

The only time I got all five spellings right in the test – I copied off Clever Clare.

For weeks I sneaked my homework into the recycling box and didn't do any of it. Unfortunately, Dad found it all in the end.

Nits love me – they have parties on my head!

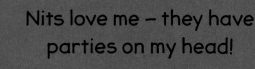

During the school trip to the Old Town Museum, I fell and set off the burglar alarms. But it was Peter who got the blame. It was brilliant!

I know the secret place where Peter hides his pocket money: in his cello case, tee hee!

I can burp to the theme tune of one of my favourite programmes, Marvin the Maniac. I'm even better at burping than Rude Ralph!

On Mother's Day, I gave Mum a beautiful bunch of tulips. Little did she know I'd picked them from our garden.

I've already written my will – and I left Peter my sweet wrappers and a muddy twig, ha ha!

Guess what I do with all the useless, horrible presents I've ever been given? I hide them in a big box under my bed and they are never seen again!

Pssst! Perfect Peter has a few sneaky little secrets to tell you about Henry too.

Henry is scared of chickens. What a big baby!

New Nick's little sister, Lisping Lily, wants to marry him, tee hee!

Mum makes Henry wear Stuck-up Steve's cast-off clothes.

He keeps a secret sweet tin under his bed (and he thinks nobody knows).

I lost my first tooth before Henry.

Henry is terrified of Milksop Miles's giant happy nappy.

Brainy Brian's Brainbusting Party Games

It's Horrid Henry's birthday party. Henry just wants to play with his new Goo-Shooter and splatter his guests in green goo. So Brainy Brian suggests some games that everyone will enjoy (especially if you're brainy!).

THE 5 CHANGE CHALLENGE

YOU WILL NEED

Two teams

HOW TO PLAY

1. Team 1 leaves the room

2. Team 2 moves five of the objects in the room (you can turn the objects upside down, back to front or to a different place)

3. Team 1 returns and tries to spot the five changes, in a time limit of five minutes

4. The teams then swap round, so that Team 2 leaves the room and Team 1 makes the five changes

5. Whichever team guesses the most changes is the winner!

> **BRAINY BRIAN'S TOP TIP:**
> Don't play this game somewhere messy, like Horrid Henry's room, as it's impossible to spot what's been changed!

TOPS AND BOTTOMS

YOU WILL NEED

A pencil and a piece of paper for each player

HOW TO PLAY

1. One of the other players chooses a category. It could be food, colours, toys, sport – or whatever you like

2. Let's say that Brainy Brian has chosen food as the category. Each player writes down their favourite food – their top – and the food they hate the most – their bottom. Then all the players give their papers to Brainy Brian

3. Brainy Brian reads the papers out loud. The other players have to guess who wrote what. You can't guess your own, of course!

4. The player who guesses the most correctly is the winner!

> CATEGORY – FOOD
>
> TOP – I dunno
>
> BOTTOM – Dunno

Beefy Bert's Birthday Games

Beefy Bert thinks Brainy Brian's games are far too tricky.
His games are much easier to play and lots of fun!

BIFF THE BAG

YOU WILL NEED

A large paper bag filled with (wrapped-up) sweets
An adult to attach the bag to a tree branch or a door frame
A stick
Enough scarves to blindfold each player

HOW TO PLAY

1. Use the scarves to blindfold all the players

2. Each player takes a turn and tries to hit the bag of sweets with the stick

3. The player who bursts the bag wins all the sweets!

HILARIOUS HATS

YOU WILL NEED

A large bag or basket full of funny old hats
A ball
Enough scarves to blindfold each player
Someone to play music for the game

HOW TO PLAY

1. All the players sit in a circle. Use the scarves to blindfold each player

2. The big bag of hats is placed in the middle of the circle

3. The players pass the ball round the circle while the music plays

4. When the music stops, the player who is holding the ball has to pick out a hat and put it on

5. The game is over when all the players have picked out a hat. The players remove their blindfolds – and get to see what everyone looks like in their funny hats!

Are You Like
Brainy Brian or Beefy Bert?

This quiz is all about Horrid Henry and his friends and enemies.
Tick YES, NO or I DUNNO and see if you can match Brainy Brian's
brilliant score or end up like Beefy Bert with a big fat zero.

1. Does Henry like eating snails?

YES ☐   NO ☐   I DUNNO ☐

2. Is Perfect Peter's club called the Big Bad Boys' Club?

YES ☐   NO ☐   I DUNNO ☐

3. Did Moody Margaret win the Frosty Freeze
Best Snowman competition with her Ballerina Snowgirl?

YES ☐   NO ☐   I DUNNO ☐

4. Was Perfect Peter chosen to play Joseph
in the school Christmas play?

YES ☐   NO ☐   I DUNNO ☐

5. Did Rabid Rebecca, the babysitter, get Rude Ralph
to bed at six o'clock?

YES ☐   NO ☐   I DUNNO ☐

6. When Lazy Linda screams, is it the loudest noise anyone has ever heard?

YES ☐   NO ☐   I DUNNO ☐

7. Does Lisping Lily want to give Perfect Peter a big kiss?

YES ☐   NO ☐   I DUNNO ☐

8. Did Bossy Bill photocopy his own bottom at his dad's work?

YES ☐   NO ☐   I DUNNO ☐

Vote Henry OR ELSE!

9. Did Horrid Henry get more votes than Moody Margaret in the School Council President election?

YES ☐   NO ☐   I DUNNO ☐

10. Is Tidy Ted one of Horrid Henry's best friends?

YES ☐   NO ☐   I DUNNO ☐

10 – Brilliant!	**6-9 Well done!**	**1-5 Oh dear –**	**0 Uh-oh!**
You've scored full marks. You're definitely more like Brainy Brian than Beefy Bert, so go straight to the top of the class.	You're not a total brainbox like Brainy Brian, but you're still a long way from being a Beefy Bert.	This poor score reveals that you're much more like Beefy Bert than Brainy Brian. Quick, have another go and see if you can score more!	This score is as low as you can go! It must mean that you gave all the wrong answers or, just like Beefy Bert, you always ticked "I DUNNO"!

Check out the answers on page 74

Brainy Brian's Pancake Pattern Puzzle

Can you solve Brainy Brian's pancake pattern puzzles below by working out which picture comes next in each sequence? Draw the correct picture in each box or write the letter a, b, c or d, as shown below.

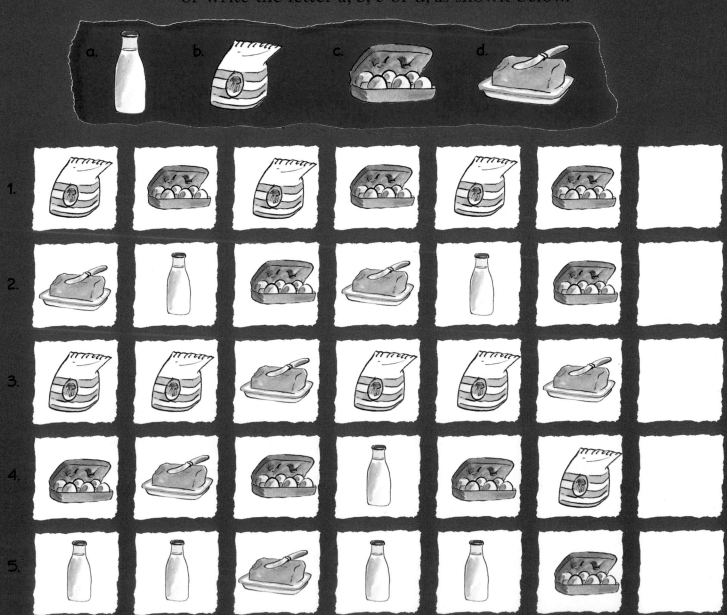

The answers are on page 74

Moody Margaret's School

"Pay attention, Susan," shrieked Moody Margaret, "or you'll go straight to the head."

"I am paying attention," said Sour Susan.

"This is boring," said Horrid Henry. "I want to play pirates."

"Silence," said Moody Margaret, whacking her ruler on the table.

"I want to be the teacher," said Susan.

"No," said Margaret.

"I'll be the teacher," said Horrid Henry. He'd send the class straight out for play-time, and tell them to run for their lives.

"Are you out of your mind?" snapped Margaret.

"Can I be the teacher?" asked Perfect Peter.

"NO!" shouted Margaret, Susan and Henry.

"Why can't I be the head?" said Susan sourly.

"Because," said Margaret.

"'cause why?" said Susan.

"'cause I'm the head."

"But you're the head and the teacher," said Susan. "It's not fair."

"It is too fair, 'cause you'd make a terrible head," said Margaret.

"Wouldn't!"

"Would!"

"I think we should take turns being head," said Susan.

"That," said Margaret, "is the dumbest idea I've ever heard. Do you see

Mrs Oddbod taking turns being head? I don't think so."

Margaret's class grumbled mutinously on the carpet inside the Secret Club tent.

"Class, I will now take the register," intoned Margaret. "Susan?"

"Here."

"Peter?"

"Here."

"Henry?"

"In the toilet."

Margaret scowled.

"We'll try that again. Henry?"

"Flushed away."

"Last chance," said Margaret severely. "Henry?"

"Dead."

Margaret made a big cross in her register. "I will deal with you later."

"No one made you the big boss," muttered Horrid Henry.

"It's my house and we'll play what I want," said Moody Margaret. "And I want to play school."

Horrid Henry scowled. Whenever Margaret came to his house she was the guest and he had to play what she wanted. But whenever Henry went to her house Margaret was the boss 'cause it was her house.

Ugggh. Why oh why did he have to live next door to Moody Margaret?

How does Henry get out of playing schools with Moody Margaret?
Find out in 'Moody Margaret's School' from *Horrid Henry Robs the Bank*.

All About ~~Me~~ THE WORLD'S MOST HORRIBLE GIRL
by Moody Margaret

I've chosen to write about the most fascinating and fantastic person in the world – ME.

When I'm asked to describe myself in three words, I always say – BEAUTIFUL, BRAVE, BEST.

What about BOSSY!!!!

Here I am being pampered by my devoted slave, and looking ~~BEAUTIFUL~~ LIKE A FROG

On the ugly scale of 1 to 10, with 1 being the ugliest, wartiest, toad, you're a 2.

My BRAVERY is famous throughout the world. When Henry put a spider on my arm, I laughed. I'm not even scared of the nit nurse (unlike scaredy-pants Henry, ha ha).

Of course I'm the BEST. Even Henry admitted it when he had to kneel down before me and beg for forgiveness.

This is a BIG FAT LIE you old bossyboots!!

THINGS I LIKE –
Getting my own way
Being first

Miss Battle-Axe asks her class to write about something they find fascinating for homework. Moody Margaret chooses to write about herself.

24

To prove I'm the BEST, here are just a few of the things that I'm brilliant at – there are loads more, of course.

GETTING MY OWN WAY – It's easy. If I'm in someone else's house, I say – "I'm the guest so you have to do what I want." If I'm in my own house, I say – "It's my house so you have to do what I want."

SCREAMING – I can scream longer and louder than anyone else.

PLAYING THE TRUMPET – I do this very loudly too, and I always practise at six o'clock in the morning.

LEADING THE SECRET CLUB TO VICTORY – I'm a born leader and a brilliant plotter. That's why the Secret Club always defeats the puny Purple Hand Gang.

THE PURPLE HAND GANG RULES!

AND I'M BRILLIANT AT LOADS OF OTHER THINGS TOO – like, I'm the best football player ever and the Captain of the School Football Team. I'm the most talented actor in school too, and I was, of course, chosen for the starring role of Mary in the Christmas play. I'm a demon player at Gotcha, and I can even stick my tongue out further than anyone else in the world.

HOORAY FOR ME!!

But who's been sneaking a peek at her notebook at school . . . and adding a few comments of their own!?

Finding Frogface

'Frogface' is one of Horrid Henry favourite names for Moody Margaret.
Look up, down, across and diagonally and see how many times you can you find
the word FROGFACE in the wordsearch puzzle below.

E	E	C	A	F	G	O	R	F
C	E	C	A	F	G	O	R	F
A	E	C	A	F	G	O	R	F
F	P	O	N	F	G	O	G	Y
G	E	C	A	F	G	O	R	F
O	P	A	A	F	N	O	T	S
R	P	C	A	I	M	P	R	L
F	E	C	A	F	G	O	R	F
E	E	C	A	F	G	O	R	F

Write down the leftover letters in the spaces below. Moody Margaret calls Horrid Henry
one of these in her newspaper, *The Daily Dagger*.

‒ ‒ ‒ ‒ ‒   ‒ ‒ ‒ ‒ ‒

Moody Margaret's Best Mum Trophy

Moody Margaret decides to make her mum a Best Mum Trophy for Mother's Day.
Except she turns it into a Best Daughter Trophy instead!

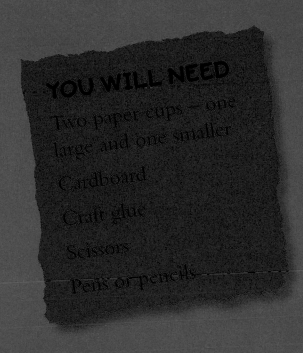

YOU WILL NEED

Two paper cups — one
large and one smaller

Cardboard

Craft glue

Scissors

Pens or pencils

WHAT TO DO

1. Glue the two cups so that their
bottoms are attached together.
The smaller cup becomes the base of
the trophy.

2. Cut two identical circles out of the
cardboard to make the handles.

to start
the handles

3. Fold one of the circles in half.

4. On one half of this circle, draw and
cut out a handle shape, as shown.

folded
with hole
cut out

5. Glue the other half of the circle to
the larger cup, to create a handle.

6. Repeat with the second circle to
make another handle.

fold solid
part in
half

7. Glue the second handle to the cup
opposite the first handle.

cups

8. In your best handwriting, write 'Best
Mum' on the front of the trophy.

Rude Ralph's Guide to Being Rude

Rude Ralph is even ruder than Horrid Henry!
Here's his step-by-step guide to being really rude.***

***WARNING: If you follow in Rude Ralph's footsteps, your teacher will make you do 10 hours of homework every night and your parents will ban you from watching TV for 100 years.

2. NEVER BE POLITE

Words like "please" and "thank you" are wormy words, and are only used by polite goody-goodies like Perfect Peter. NEVER say these words.

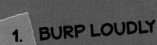

1. BURP LOUDLY

Burping is VERY rude. To become a Champion Burper, like me, burp as loudly and as often as possible.

Top Tip:
Drink a can of Fizzywizz very fast before you burp.

3. TELL LOTS OF RUDE JOKES

Rude jokes are the funniest. Here's my favourite:
Why did the toilet roll down the hill?
It wanted to get to the bottom!

5. SHOUT OUT RUDE NAMES

Calling people rude names is fun. Here are some of my best rude name-calling names; poo breath, smellovision and wibble pants (OK, Henry called me that one!)

4. BE A BAD GUEST

When your friends' parents give you horrible stuff to eat, like cauliflower cheese, DON'T eat it.
Say: **"Bleccch! – I'm not eating this!"**

6. BOAST A LOT

If you get a new toy – boast about it to everyone and make them all jealous!

Are You as Rude as Rude Ralph?

Follow this flowchart to find out if you're as rude as Rude Ralph.

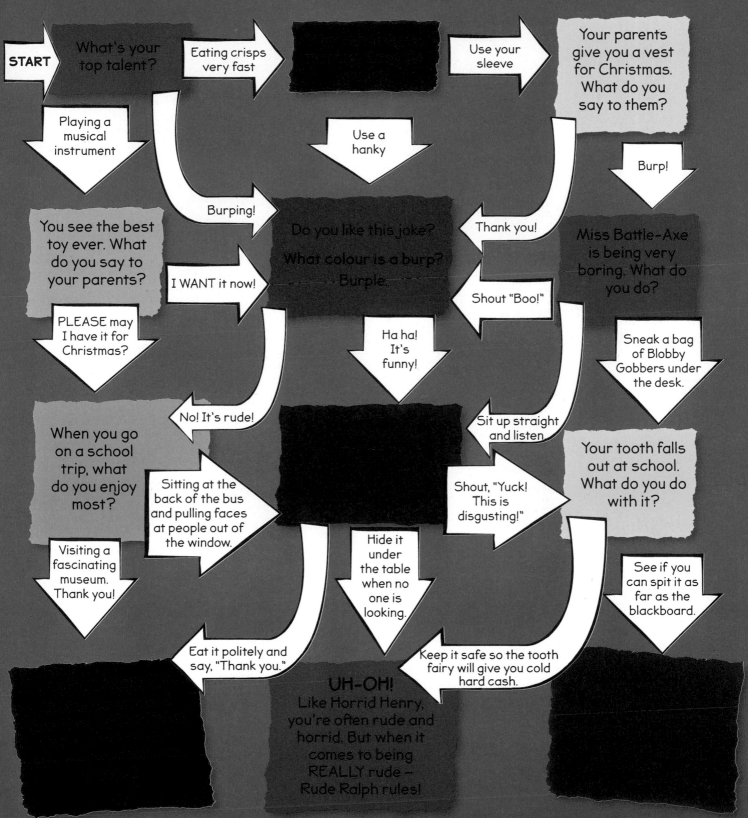

START

What's your top talent?

Eating crisps very fast

Use your sleeve

Your parents give you a vest for Christmas. What do you say to them?

Playing a musical instrument

Use a hanky

Burp!

Burping!

You see the best toy ever. What do you say to your parents?

I WANT it now!

Do you like this joke?
What colour is a burp?
— Burple.

Thank you!

Miss Battle-Axe is being very boring. What do you do?

PLEASE may I have it for Christmas?

Shout "Boo!"

Ha ha! It's funny!

Sneak a bag of Blobby Gobbers under the desk.

No! It's rude!

Sit up straight and listen

When you go on a school trip, what do you enjoy most?

Sitting at the back of the bus and pulling faces at people out of the window.

Shout, "Yuck! This is disgusting!"

Your tooth falls out at school. What do you do with it?

Visiting a fascinating museum. Thank you!

Hide it under the table when no one is looking.

See if you can spit it as far as the blackboard.

Eat it politely and say, "Thank you."

UH-OH!
Like Horrid Henry, you're often rude and horrid. But when it comes to being REALLY rude – Rude Ralph rules!

Keep it safe so the tooth fairy will give you cold hard cash.

April Fool's Day Tricks

It's the Purple Hand Gang versus the Secret Club on April Fool's Day. Here are the best tricks the Purple Hand Gang have played:

Secret Club Biscuit Tin Trick

1. On a piece of paper, Horrid Henry wrote a note:
   Nah nah ne nah nah! April Fool's!!!!
   The Purple Hand Gang rules!!
2. Rude Ralph and Horrid Henry sneaked into the Secret Club Tent.
3. They pinched their secret stash of cookies and replaced them with Henry's note.
4. Then they sneaked off and scoffed all the biscuits!

Rude Ralph's Minty Molars

1. Rude Ralph munched on a mint – but didn't swallow it.
2. He barged rudely into the Secret Club Tent. Moody Margaret gave him a big shove, and Ralph pretended to be hurt. He wailed and clutched his mouth – then spat out the pieces of broken mint.
3. Moody Margaret and Sour Susan thought he'd broken his teeth!

You could play this trick at home by leaving a note in the biscuit tin or sweetie jar, and hiding all the sweets and biscuits.

All you need are some mints, and you can play this trick too.

Secret Club Tent Terrors

1. Henry and Ralph hid their horrible hairy hairbrushes in the Secret Club Tent.
2. As Margaret and Susan snuggled down to whisper some secret plans, they felt something hairy nibbling at their toes. AAAAAgh!!!!
3. As they ran screaming from the tent, Henry and Ralph were waiting outside. April Fools!!

You can play this trick at home by hiding your hairbrush in your little brother or sister's bed.

But the Secret Club always take their revenge with their own sneaky tricks...

Bouncing Bunch of Bananas

1. Sour Susan tied a bunch of bananas onto a tree using a length of elastic.
2. Moody Margaret told Henry and Ralph about a tree in her garden that grows bananas. They thought she was telling a big fat fib – so she dared them to pick the bananas.
3. When they tried, the bananas sprang back on the elastic!
4. Margaret and Susan collapsed into giggles, screaming, "April Fool's!!!"

Tearaway Trousers

1. Margaret pretended to drop a few coins on the pavement outside her house, and then hid behind a hedge with Susan.
2. Henry spotted the coins and went to pinch the cold hard cash.
3. As he bent over to pick them up, Margaret tore an old rag as loudly as she could – and Susan screeched, "Poopy pants!"
4. Henry thought his trousers had ripped!

All you need are a few coins and an old rag and you can play this trick anywhere there's a good hiding place.

Ask an adult to help you tie some bananas to a tree in your garden, and then you can fool a friend too.

April Fool's Ice Cream

1. Sour Susan made an ice cream sundae, but she used cold leftover mashed potato instead of ice cream, and cold gravy for the sauce! She sprinkled it with sweets to make it look yummy.
2. Susan put her sundae in the Secret Club Tent for the Purple Hand Gang to find.
3. When Horrid Henry and Rude Ralph saw the ice cream, they tucked in straight away – and bleccchh!! – soon realised they'd been well and truly tricked!

Could you create your own April Fool's Day ice cream sundae with some leftovers?

Which club do you think had the best tricks on April Fool's Day?

START

Easter Egg Hunt Maze

Help Moody Margaret and Sour Susan find the right path through the maze.

Make sure you pass 10 Easter eggs along the way, and don't go near Rude Ralph's Rotten Egg Stinkbombs!

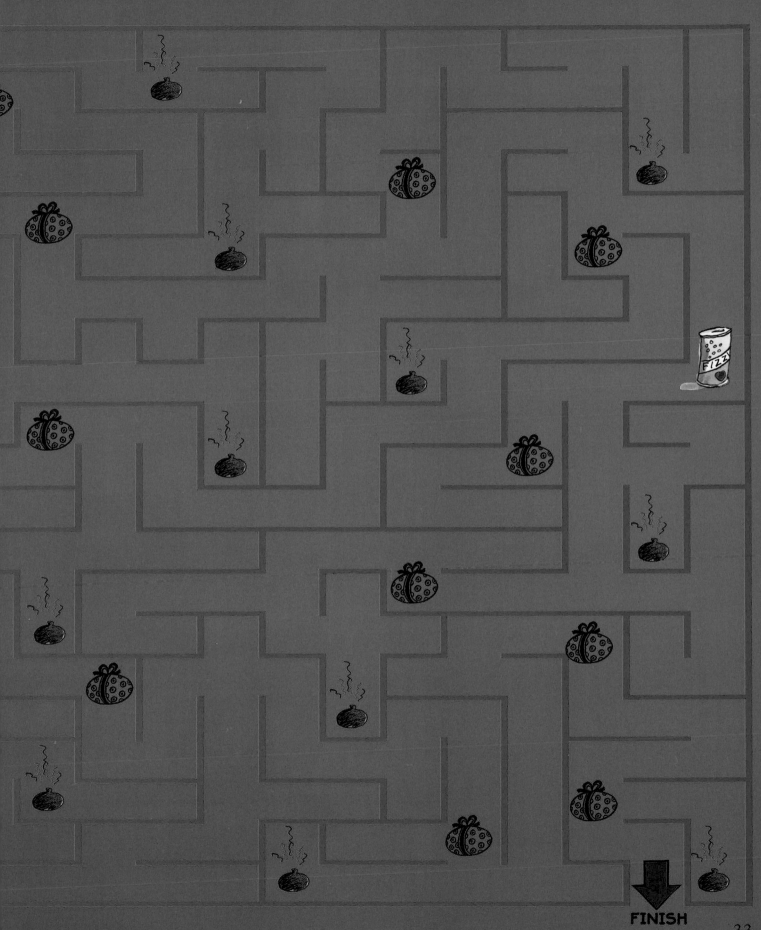

FINISH

33

Are You As Good As Gold?

Perfect Peter always has the most stars in the
Good as Gold Book at school.

Could you earn as many stars as Perfect Peter?
Find out by ticking your answers
in the boxes below.

1. Is your school report perfect?

YES ☐   SOMETIMES ☐   NO ☐

2. Do you do your homework as soon as you get home from school?

YES ☐   SOMETIMES ☐   NO ☐

3. Do you wash and comb your hair every night so that you never get nits?

YES ☐   SOMETIMES ☐   NO ☐

4. Do you love eating vegetables?

YES ☐   SOMETIMES ☐   NO ☐

5. Do you enjoy helping Mum and Dad do the housework?

YES ☐   SOMETIMES ☐   NO ☐

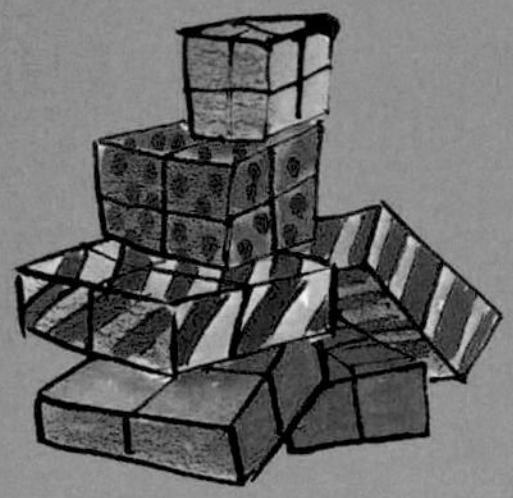

6. Do you write your thank you letters as soon as you've opened your presents?

YES ☐ SOMETIMES ☐ NO ☐

7. Do you say NO to snacking between meals?

YES ☐ SOMETIMES ☐ NO ☐

8. Do you love long walks in the countryside?

YES ☐ SOMETIMES ☐ NO ☐

9. Do you keep your bedroom clean and tidy?

YES ☐ SOMETIMES ☐ NO ☐

10. Do you like to go to bed early?

YES ☐ SOMETIMES ☐ NO ☐

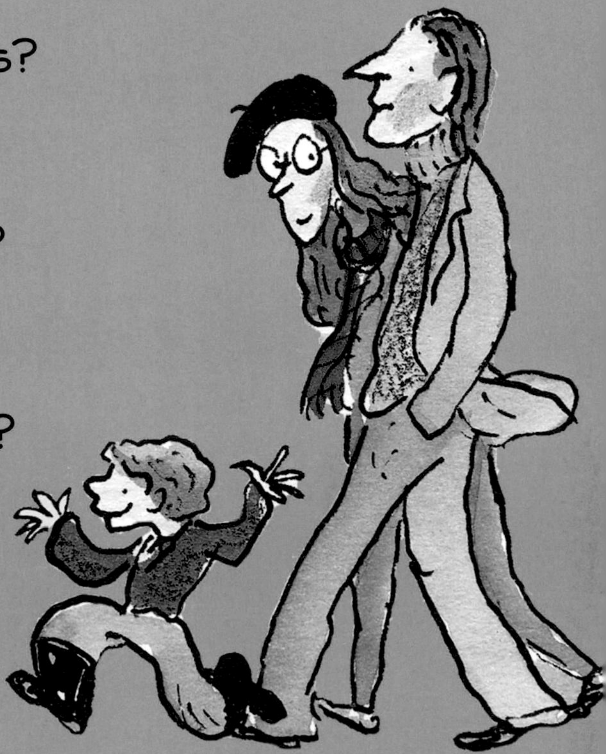

It's time to count up your score!

For every **YES** you ticked – award yourself **1 STAR**
For every **SOMETIMES** you ticked – score **nothing**
For every **NO** you ticked – **take off 1 STAR**

How did you do?

10 STARS

Unbelievable! You're as perfect as Perfect Peter and earn a very well-deserved place next to him in the Good as Gold Book.

6–9 STARS

A great score but it's not quite a perfect 10. If you want to be the best, take a tip from Perfect Peter and be a goody-goody ALL the time.

1–5 STARS

You've a long way to go before you achieve the most stars in the Good as Gold Book. But you've earned at least one star – which is loads better than . . .

. . . ZERO OR MINUS STARS!

You are banned from the Good as Gold Book!! You must be as lazy as Lazy Linda! Or as rude as Rude Ralph! Or even aaagh! – as horrid as Horrid Henry!

Horrid Henry and the Mad Professor

Chocolate, here I come, thought Horrid Henry, heaving his bones and dashing over to his skeleton bank. He shook it. Then he shook it again. There wasn't even a rattle.

How could have no money and no sweets? It was so unfair! Just last night Peter had been boasting about having £7.48 in his piggy bank. And loads of sweets left over from Hallowe'en. Horrid Henry scowled. Why did Peter always have money? Why did he, Henry, never have money?

Money was totally wasted on Peter. What was the point of Peter having pocket money since he never spent it? Come to think of it, what was the point of Peter having sweets since he never ate them?

There was a shuffling, scuttling noise, then Perfect Peter dribbled into Henry's bedroom carrying all his soft toys.

"Get out of my room, worm!" bellowed Horrid Henry, holding his nose. "You're stinking it up."

"I am not," said Peter.

"Are too, smelly pants."

"I do not have smelly pants," said Peter.

"Do too, woofy, poofy, pongy pants."

Peter opened his mouth, then closed it.

"Henry, will you play with me?" said Peter.

"No."

"Please?"

"No!"

"Pretty please?"

"No!!"

"But we could play school with all my cuddly toys," said Peter. "Or have a tea party with them …"

"For the last time, NOOOOOOO!" screamed Horrid Henry.

"You never play with me," said Perfect Peter.

"That's 'cause you're a toad-faced nappy wibble bibble," said Horrid Henry. "Now go away and leave me alone."

"Mum! Henry's calling me names again!" screamed Peter. "He called me wibble bibble."

"Henry! Don't be horrid!" shouted Mum.

Do Henry and Peter play together in the end – and what do they play?
Find out in 'Horrid Henry and the Mad Professor' from *Horrid Henry and the Zombie Vampire*.

Perfect Peter's Picture Puzzle

Can you spot the six differences in the two pictures?

1. _____

2. _____

3. _____

4. _____

5. _____

6. _____

37

Perfect Peter's Spring Worm Watch

Peter is worm,
Peter is worm,
Peter is a Wor

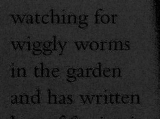

Peter has been watching for wiggly worms in the garden and has written lots of fascinating facts about them in his nature notebook.

EVERYTHING I KNOW ABOUT WORMS
by Peter, May 2017

 Worms don't like light. The best time to watch for worms is in springtime, on warm, damp evenings. Mum and Dad let me stay up past my bedtime when I'm worm watching.

 Even when worms are underground, they know when it's raining.

Dad says worms are good for the garden because they make channels in the soil, letting water, plant roots and air move through.

Worms are covered with hundreds of tiny bristles to help them grip as they wriggle along their tunnels.

 Worms eat their own weight in food each day.

Worms eat all sorts of things, like dead leaves, cardboard, vegetables and tea bags.

 Worms are strong. When I held one gently in my fist, I could feel it trying to push its way out through my fingers.

 Their favourite food is melon rind.

 If you cut a worm in two close to the end of its tail (the fatter pink piece), the worm will regrow a new tail. But if you cut the worm in half anywhere else, it will die.

 When it's hot in the summer, worms sometimes curl up and have a snooze.

 Worms can live from several months to as long as ten years.

 A plot 10 metres x 10 metres – about the size of my classroom at school – contains about 2,500 worms.

MY MOST AMAZING FACT

 The giant African Earthworm from South Africa is nearly 7 metres long – that's longer than three skipping ropes tied together – but only about as thick as my finger.

THESE ARE THE MOST BORING FACTS EVER!

HERE ARE MY MUCH MORE INTERESTING FACTS ABOUT THE WORMIEST WORM OF ALL!

- Perfect Peter still wears nappies
- Perfect Peter is a wibble bibble poopy pants
- Perfect Peter is a crybaby

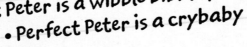

TOP TIP!
Fill in the two longest words first.

Sour Susan's Criss-Cross

Can you solve Sour Susan's criss-cross puzzle by slotting in all her sour S words.

3 letters
SLY

4 letters
SOUR

5 letters
SHARP
SULKY
SURLY

6 letters
SNAPPY
SULLEN
SHIFTY
SNEAKY

8 letters
SPITEFUL

9 letters
SECRETIVE

40

Sour Susan's Sour Sudoku

Fill in the sudoku so that every square and row – both up and down – contains a picture of Sour Susan, a lemon, a stinkbomb and a gooseberry.

TOP TIP!
Fill in the 3's and the 6's first.

Too easy-peasy for you? Try a trickier sudoku!

Fill in every square and row with numbers 1-6.

The answers are on page 75

41

Sour Susan's Secret Seven Code

When Sour Susan wants to send a secret message to Moody Margaret, she uses her Secret Seven Code.

1. Susan wants to send a message in code to Margaret to say 'HENRY HAS HIDDEN GOOEY CHEWIES IN HIS FORT.'

On a piece of paper, she draws a grid with SEVEN ROWS. Then she writes her message in COLUMNS from top to bottom, like this:

					TOP
1	H	S	G	E	H
2	E	H	O	W	I
3	N	I	O	I	S
4	R	D	E	E	F
5	Y	D	Y	S	O
6	H	E	C	I	R
7	A	N	H	N	T

LEFT → RIGHT ROWS

BOTTOM COLUMNS

2. Now Susan is ready to turn her message into code. On another piece of paper, she writes down the letters from the seven rows, left to right. Each row looks like a weird word, like this:

HSGEH EHOWI NIOIS RDEEF YDYSO HECIR ANHNT

3. Margaret knows that the Code Cracker is SEVEN. When she gets the message, she writes the words in her own SEVEN ROW grid. Now Margaret can uncode the message by reading each column from top to bottom.

Here is Margaret's message back to Susan:

SAT NNH EDE AGM KRN IAO NBW

Can you work out what she has written, using the Code Cracker of SEVEN. Use the grid if it helps!

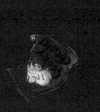

1			
2			
3			
4			
5			
6			
7			

Best Friends with Moody Margaret

Would you be a good best friend for Margaret — or would you make a better enemy? Follow the flow chart and find out!

Start here

Do you think that Margaret is a moody old grouch?

yes → Does Margaret look like a frog?

yes → Are you brave enough to call Margaret "frogface" when she can hear you?

sometimes → Are you as moody and mean as Margaret is herself?

no (from Margaret moody grouch) → Would you be grumpy if Margaret found another best friend?

no (from frog) → Would you dare mutter "meanie" at Margaret under your breath.

yes (from brave enough) → Would you storm off in a sulk if Moody Margaret called you a "blabbermouth"?

Are you as moody and mean as Margaret is herself? → *no* → Would you be grumpy if Margaret found another best friend?

Would you be grumpy if Margaret found another best friend? → *yes* → Would you dare mutter "meanie" at Margaret under your breath.

Would you dare mutter "meanie" at Margaret under your breath → *yes* (from storm off) ← Would you storm off in a sulk if Moody Margaret called you a "blabbermouth"?

yes (from Are you as moody) → Could you be a brilliant and sneaky super-spy?

yes (from grumpy) →

Would you ever tell on Margaret to your teacher?

no (from mutter meanie) → If Margaret invited you to a sleepover, would you go?

no (from blabbermouth) → Would you rather marry Miss Battle-Axe than Moody Margaret?

Could you be a brilliant and sneaky super-spy? → *no* → Would you ever tell on Margaret to your teacher?

Would you ever tell on Margaret to your teacher? → *no* → If Margaret invited you to a sleepover, would you go?

If Margaret invited you to a sleepover, would you go? → *no* → Would you rather marry Miss Battle-Axe than Moody Margaret?

Could you be a brilliant and sneaky super-spy? → *yes* → Would you be prepared to spy for a rival gang and double-cross a best friend?

Would you ever tell on Margaret to your teacher? → *yes* →

If Margaret invited you to a sleepover, would you go? → *yes* →

Would you rather marry Miss Battle-Axe than Moody Margaret? → *yes* → Would you dare to try and stinkbomb the Secret Club?

Would you be prepared to spy for a rival gang and double-cross a best friend? → *no* →

→ *no* → Would you dare to try and stinkbomb the Secret Club?

Would you be prepared to spy for a rival gang and double-cross a best friend? → *yes* → If you and Margaret fell out, would you make friends again if she made you Chief Spy of the Club?

sometimes → Do you think that Margaret is OK, but you've already got lots of best friends?

Would you dare to try and stinkbomb the Secret Club? → *yes* → Do you think Moody Margaret should be dumped in a bin?

If you and Margaret fell out, would you make friends again if she made you Chief Spy of the Club? → *no* → Do you think that Margaret is OK, but you've already got lots of best friends?

Do you think that Margaret is OK, but you've already got lots of best friends? → *no* →

Do you think Moody Margaret should be dumped in a bin? → *no* →

If you and Margaret fell out, would you make friends again if she made you Chief Spy of the Club? → *yes* → **Like Sour Susan, you're a grumpy, double-crossing sneak – and the perfect best friend for Moody Margaret.**

Do you think that Margaret is OK, but you've already got lots of best friends? → *yes* → **Like Gorgeous Gurinder or Lazy Linda, you sometimes let Margaret boss you about – but only when she's sharing her Chocolate Spitballs with you.**

Do you think Moody Margaret should be dumped in a bin? → *yes* → **Like Horrid Henry, you think Margaret is the most horrible girl in the world – and you are destined to be sworn enemies for ever.**

Horrid Henry's Gruesome Grown-Ups

School has finished for the summer and Henry can escape Miss Battle-Axe at last. But there are some gruesome grown-ups he can't get away from . . .

DAD

Makes me eat vegetables

Blames me and never Peter

Doesn't give me £1,000 pocket money a day

Thinks walks are healthy

Ideal holiday:

Staying in a cabin with no electricity or running water (uggh!!!)

MUM

Shouts all the time

Never lets me watch as much telly as I want

Makes me do my homework

Blames me and never Peter

Doesn't give me £1,000 pocket money a day

Ideal summer holiday:

In a library

PRISSY POLLY

Being prissy

Keeping Vera instead of sending her straight to prison where she belongs

Ideal holiday:
Anywhere with a full-time baby crèche

PIMPLY PAUL

Being pimply and hating children

Bringing Vera to Henry's house

Ideal holiday:
Anywhere with a full-time baby crèche

RICH AUNT RUBY

Gives horrible presents like lime green cardigans instead of money

Gave birth to that snake, Stuck-Up Steve

GREAT AUNT GRETA

Can never remember that I'm a boy, not a girl

Gives terrible presents like pink underpants and burping dolls

Ideal holiday:
Staying at home

Ideal holiday:
A cruise on a golden ship

SCHOOL'S OUT FOR **SUMMER**

Who's Who Holiday Crossword

This giant crossword will keep you busy over the summer holidays. Check out the picture clues and fit in your favourite characters' names.

3 across

5 across

6 across

9 across

12 across

15 across

13 across

14 across

1 down

7 down

2 down

4 down

8 down

10 down

11 down

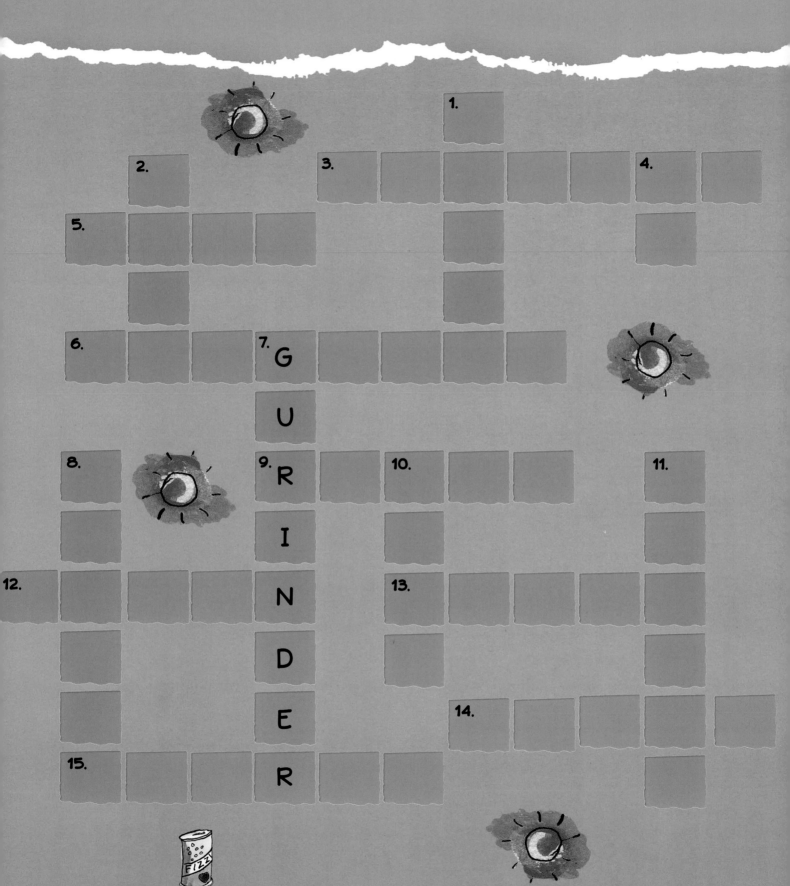

The answer to Clue 7 Down has been filled in for you already.
Check your answers on page 75.

Jolly Josh's Holiday Howlers

Why do bananas wear suncream?
Because they peel.

Why was Greedy Graham doing the backstroke after lunch?
Because you aren't supposed to swim on a full stomach.

Why did the monkey sunbathe?
To get an orangu-tan.

Who wears the biggest sun hat?
The person with the biggest head.

Knock knock.
Who's there?
Summer.
Summer who?
Summer better than others at telling jokes.

What do you call a snowman in July?

A puddle.

What's black and white and red all over?

A zebra with sunburn. Ouch!

What happens when you throw a yellow pebble into the blue sea?

It sinks.

What do sheep do on sunny days?

Have a baa-baa-cue.

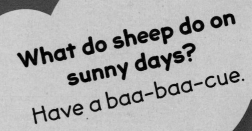

NITTY NORA: Where do nits go on holiday?
HORRID HENRY: Search me.

Why didn't Beefy Bert enjoy his water-skiing holiday?

He couldn't find a sloping lake.

What's the best day to go to the beach?

SUNday.

Perfect Peter's
Paper and Pencil Page

There's plenty of time for games in the long summer holidays,
and Jolly Josh is looking for someone to play with.
Perfect Peter is thrilled when Josh agrees to join in his favourite game.
It's a bit like noughts and crosses – with lots of rubbing out!

YOU WILL NEED

Two players
Paper, pencil and a rubber

THE RULES

1. You play the game on a grid of squares. It's best to start with a grid of 3, but you can go as big as you like!

2. The younger player goes first and chooses 0's or X's.

3. To start with, each player puts two 0's and two X's in the corners of the grid.

4. The game begins, and each player makes a move in turn.

5. You move by adding your symbol in a square next to one you already have. You can move upwards, downwards or side to side, but NOT diagonally.

6. When you have made your move, your opponent loses any of the squares next to your new square. When losing squares, 'next to' means upwards, downwards, side to side AND diagonally. You rub out your opponent's symbols and add in your own.

7. The game continues until all the squares are filled, or one of the players has lost all his symbols and can no longer make a move.

8. The winner is the player with the most symbols in the grid at the end of the game.

50

Can you follow Perfect Peter and Jolly's Josh's game?
The symbols in red show the next moves.

1. Peter draws a neat grid of 3 squares by 3 squares.

2. Peter is 0's and he goes first by adding two 0's in two of the corners.

3. Josh puts his two X's in the remaining two corners.

4. Peter moves.

5. Peter rubs out Josh's X and replaces it with a 0.

6. Josh moves.

7. Josh rubs out Peter's 0 and replaces it with a X.

8. Peter moves. Good move, Peter!

9. Jolly Josh loses all his X's, and Perfect Peter wins the game.

51

How To Win at Everything
An Acrostic Poem by Aerobic Al

A hundred push-ups before breakfast

E xercise every day

R un like a bolt of lightning

O nly the whitest of white trainers will do
for me

B e fit, be fast, be fantastic!

I nsult opponents to put them off – like,
"Go home and take a nap, Henry!"

C onfident, cool and calm – that's me!

A im high – it's the way to win

L ose is a word I never use!

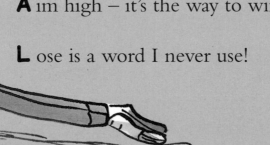

Can you write an acrostic poem using your own name?

Aerobic Al's Road Run

Aerobic Al sets out from his house in the morning for a run.
He wants to run as far as possible without going down the same street twice –
and get back home for his breakfast. Can you work how he can do this?

Start and finish at Al's house

One possible route is shown in the answers on page 76.

Aerobic Al's Summer Challenges

Aerobic Al has set some summer challenges for his friends.
Can you beat Al's super-high scores?

CHALLENGE 1

How many marbles can you transfer from one bowl of water to another – using only your feet. *Time limit – 60 seconds.*

AEROBIC AL **20**   BRAINY BRIAN **8**

MY SCORE

CHALLENGE 2

How many dried peas can you transfer from one cup to another with a drinking straw?
Time limit – 30 seconds.

AEROBIC AL **35**   MOODY MARGARET **34**

MY SCORE

CHALLENGE 3

How many times can you hop up and down on one foot?
Time limit – 30 seconds.

AEROBIC AL **60**   GREEDY GRAHAM **10**

MY SCORE

CHALLENGE 4

How many cottonballs can you transfer from a bowl to a plate, using a spoon – and wearing a blindfold? Using two hands is cheating! *Time limit – 60 seconds.*

AEROBIC AL SOUR SUSAN MY SCORE

CHALLENGE 5

How many times can you bounce a ball on the ground? *Time limit – 30 seconds.*

AEROBIC AL RUDE RALPH

MY SCORE

CHALLENGE 6

Lay out a pile of clothing – trousers, t-shirt, jumper, shirt, coat, scarf, hat, and gloves. How many of the clothes can you put on? *Time limit – 30 seconds.*

AEROBIC AL BEEFY BERT

MY SCORE

CHALLENGE 7

Peel an orange so that there are as few pieces of peel as possible. How many pieces have you finished with? *Time limit – 30 seconds.*

AEROBIC AL HORRID HENRY

MY SCORE

Henry, we're NOT doing this. OK!

THE BEST CHALLENGE

See how many packets of crisps you can scoff. *Time limit – 10 minutes.*

AEROBIC AL 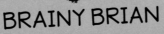 BRAINY BRIAN

55

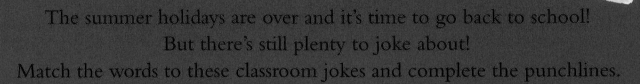

School Jokes Double Puzzle

The summer holidays are over and it's time to go back to school!
But there's still plenty to joke about!
Match the words to these classroom jokes and complete the punchlines.

4 letters	**5 letters**	**6 letters**	**7 letters**
HIGH	DRIVE	PUPILS	DINNERS
HIVE	RULER		
MOAN	SMELL		
	STICK		

1. Why did Horrid Henry take a ladder to school?

Because he wanted to go to _ _ _ _ school.

2. What's a mushroom?

The place where Greasy Greta cooks the school _ _ _ _ _ _ _.

3. How does Clever Clare get straight A's?

By using a _ _ _ _ _.

4. What did Mrs Oddbod say to the naughty bee?

Bee- _ _ _ _ yourself.

5. Why did Mr Nerdon go cross-eyed?

He couldn't control his _ _ _ _ _ _.

56

6. Why did Sour Susan take her car to school?

To _ _ _ _ _ Miss Battle-Axe up the wall.

7. Why did Beefy Bert put glue on his head?

To help things _ _ _ _ _ in his mind.

8. Why was Rude Ralph's packed lunch so stinky?

It had passed its _ _ _ _ _ -by-date.

9. What's Moody Margaret's favourite school day?

_ _ _ _ DAY.

Now fit the same words into the criss-cross puzzle too.

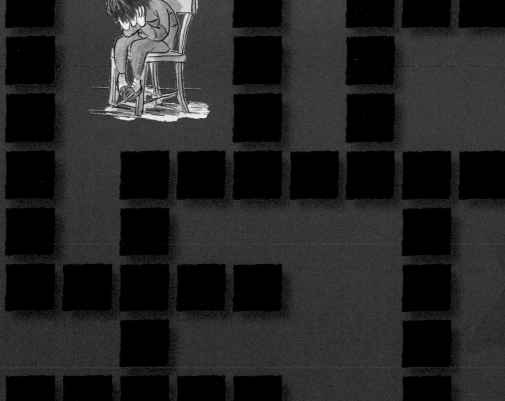

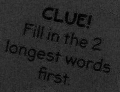

CLUE!
Fill in the 2 longest words first.

57

Beware – It's Miss Battle-Axe!

Miss Battle-Axe is the meanest teacher in the school.
If your teacher is like this too, be warned!

WATCH OUT!

Miss Battle-Axe has eyes
in the back of her head!

She's old and bony, but she spins round
faster than you can hide a bag of
Blobby Gobbers under the desk.

Don't dare cheat in the spelling test!
Those beady eyes will soon swivel over the
class and catch you copying Clever Clare.

HOW DO I KNOW
WHEN I'M IN REALLY
BIG TROUBLE?

- Miss Battle-Axe bares her fangs
- She fixes me with her steely stare
- She taps me on the shoulder
  with a long bony finger
- She smiles at me with her great
  big yellow teeth . . . And says,
  in an ice cold dagger voice . . .
  "I'm watching you, Henry."

Horrid Henry's Underpants

"Henry! Pay attention!" barked Miss Battle-Axe. "I am about to explain long division. I will only explain it once. You take a great big number, like 374, and then divide it – "

Horrid Henry was not paying attention. He was tired. He was crabby. And for some reason his pants were itchy. These pants feel horrible, he thought. And so tight. What's wrong with them?

Horrid Henry sneaked a peek.

And then Horrid Henry saw what pants he had on. Not his Driller Cannibal pants. Not his Marvin the Maniac ones either. Not even his old Gross-Out ones, with the holes and the droopy elastic.

He, Horrid Henry, was wearing frilly pink lacy girls' pants covered in glittery hearts and bows. He'd completely forgotten he'd stuffed them into his pants drawer last month so Ralph wouldn't see them. And now, oh horror of horrors, he was wearing them.

Maybe it's a nightmare, thought Horrid Henry hopefully. He pinched his arm. Ouch! Then, just to be sure he pinched William.

"Waaaaah!" wailed Weepy William.

"Stop weeping, William!" said Miss Battle-Axe. "Now, what number do I need – "

It was not a nightmare. He was still in school, still wearing pink pants.

What to do, what to do?

Don't panic, thought Horrid Henry. He took a deep breath. Don't panic. After all, no one will know. His trousers weren't see-through or anything.

Wait. What trousers was he wearing? Were there any holes in them? Quickly Horrid Henry twisted round to check his bottom.

Phew. There were no holes. What luck he hadn't put on his old jeans with the big rip but a new pair.

He was safe.

"Henry! What's the answer?" said Miss Battle-Axe.

"Pants," said Horrid Henry before he could stop himself.

The class burst out laughing.

"Pants!" screeched Rude Ralph.

"Pants!" screeched Dizzy Dave.

"Henry. Stand up," ordered Miss Battle-Axe.

Henry stood. His heart was pounding.

Aaarrrghhh! The lacy ruffle of his pink pants was showing! His new trousers were too big. Mum always bought him clothes that were way too big so he'd grow into them. These were the falling-down ones he'd tried on yesterday. Henry gripped his trousers tight and yanked them up.

"What did you say?" said Miss Battle-Axe slowly.

"Ants," said Horrid Henry.

"Ants?" said Miss Battle-Axe.

"Yeah," said Henry quickly. "I was just thinking about how many ants you could divide by – by that number you said," he added.

Miss Battle-Axe glared at him.

"I've got my eye on you, Henry," she snapped. "Now sit down and pay attention."

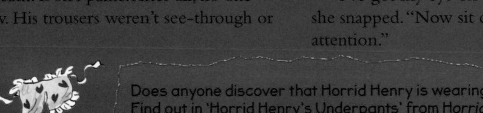

Does anyone discover that Horrid Henry is wearing pink lacy pants? Find out in 'Horrid Henry's Underpants' from *Horrid Henry's Underpants*.

MISS BATTLE-AXE'S SEPTEMBER

New Nick's Classmates Quiz

When New Nick joins the class, Miss Battle-Axe asks for a volunteer to show him around. Could you help him settle in and find out about his new classmates? Try the quiz and find out if you're up to the job.

1. Who is the biggest boy in the class?

a. Tough Toby
b. Beefy Bert
c. Brainy Brian

2. Who is the Captain of the Football Team?

a. Moody Margaret
b. Aerobic Al
c. Rude Ralph

3. Who always gets full marks in the spelling tests?

a. Singing Soraya
b. Gorgeous Gurinder
c. Clever Clare

4. Who has been caught snoring in class?

a. Lazy Linda
b. Rude Ralph
c. Greedy Graham

5. Who is the fastest runner in the class?

a. Tough Toby
b. Aerobic Al
c. Dizzy Dave

6. Who brings the biggest bags of sweets to school?

a. Beefy Bert
b. Sour Susan
c. Greedy Graham

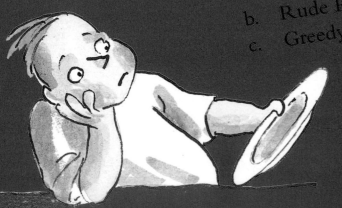

60

7. Which boy came to school wearing a pair of pink frilly knickers?

a. Anxious Andrew
b. Horrid Henry
c. Weepy William

8. Who played a blade of grass in the school Christmas play?

a. Sour Susan
b. Jolly Josh
c. Weepy William

9. Who started the craze of de-bagging – pulling people's trousers down – in the playground?

a. Horrid Henry
b. Rude Ralph
c. Moody Margaret

10. Can you match up the best friends from the following three: Rude Ralph, Beefy Bert, Clever Clare?

a. Aerobic Al _____
b. Horrid Henry _____
c. Brainy Brian _____

9 – 12

Go straight to the top of the class! If New Nick sticks with you, he'll soon find out who's fast, who's fun – and who to sit next to when there's a spelling test.

5 – 8

New Nick could learn all sorts of funny facts about his new classmates from you. But a lot of the things you tell him will be totally wrong!

0 – 4

When Miss Battle-Axe asks for a volunteer to show New Nick around, DON'T put your hand up. He'll end up in the corner of the classroom, crying with Weepy William!

Check the answers on page 76 to find out your score.

Gorgeous Gurinder's Hallowe'en Makeover Magic

Gorgeous Gurinder is face-painting her friends to look spooky and scary – all ready for trick or treating on Hallowe'en.

Horrid Henry the Vicious Vampire

INSTRUCTIONS:

1. Mix a pale shade of grey by adding black to white face paint. Use a damp sponge to cover Henry's face with paint

2. Add a few more spots of black to the paint to make a darker grey. Sponge this around Henry's eyes, and on his cheeks and chin

3. Use a paintbrush to add white fangs to Henry's mouth

4. Outline the fangs in black

5. Paint on big black eyebrows

6. Paint Henry's bottom lip red. Add drips of blood to make Henry look really vicious!

Rude Ralph
the Scary Skeleton

INSTRUCTIONS:

1. Use a damp sponge to cover Ralph's face in white face paint, including his lips
2. Circle Ralph's eyes with black face paint, and paint his cheeks to create the contours of a skull
3. Paint small black squares around Ralph's mouth

Moody Margaret the Evil Devil
INSTRUCTIONS:

1. Use a damp sponge to cover Margaret's face in red face paint
2. Add yellow highlights on Margaret's cheeks and chin
3. Use a paintbrush and black face paint for the devilish details. Paint lines around the eyes, black lips, and a pointed beard

Sour Susan the Wicked Witch

INSTRUCTIONS:

1. With a damp sponge, cover Susan's face in green face paint
2. With a paintbrush, paint her eyelids and eyebrows lilac. Also use this colour to paint a line under her eyes, and to paint her lips
3. With a paintbrush, paint Susan's eyebrows in black
4. You can also add black moons and stars to make her look really magical

Greedy Graham's Fantastic Midnight Feast

Midnight feasts are fun at a sleepover –
and Greedy Graham knows how to hold the best feasts ever!

Save up your sweets all week so there's bucketloads to share at the feast

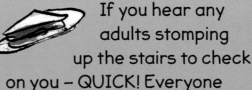

Cover your tracks the next day – by hiding the food wrappers under the bed – so the parents never find out about your fantastic secret feast!

Don't invite any scaredy-cats like Weepy William to your sleepover – they'll cry and wake up the adults – and your feast will be banned

Stay awake until midnight by playing games – but NO noise or your parents will hear you

If you hear any adults stomping up the stairs to check on you – QUICK! Everyone pretend to be asleep!

Do you think Horrid Henry and Rude Ralph are making any noise?

If you do get caught in the kitchen, smile sweetly and say that you're getting a drink of water

Don't eat crisps, crackers or cookies at your midnight feast – all that crunching might wake up the parents!

Greedy Graham's Bonfire Biscuits

Greedy Graham's recipe for chocolate sparklers is so simple that even Beefy Bert can make them!

WHAT TO DO

1. Put some hot water into a small bowl, and pour the hundreds and thousands into another small bowl

2. Dip one end of a biscuit into the hot water, so that the chocolate just melts a little, and then dip it into the hundreds and thousands

3. Carefully lay the biscuit on the greaseproof paper and leave it until the chocolate has set again

4. Do the same with the rest of the biscuits – and enjoy your chocolatey sparklers on Bonfire Night!

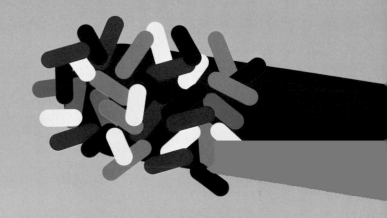

Horrid Henry's Christmas Lunch

Horrid Henry was bored. Horrid Henry was fed up. The presents had all been opened. His parents had made him go on a long, boring walk. Dad had confiscated his Terminator trident when he had speared Peter with it. So, what now?

Grandpa was sitting in the armchair with his pipe, snoring, his tinsel crown slipping over his face.

Prissy Polly and Pimply Paul were squabbling over whose turn it was to change Vera's stinky nappy.

"Eeeek," said Polly. "I did it last."

"I did," said Paul.

"WAAAAAAAAA!" wailed Vomiting Vera.

Perfect Peter was watching Sammy the Snail slithering about on TV.

Horrid Henry snatched the clicker and switched channels.

"Hey, I was watching that!" protested Peter.

"Tough," said Henry.

"Let's see, what was on? "Tra la la la …" Ick! Daffy and her Dancing Daisies.

"Wait! I want to watch!" wailed Peter. Click. "… and the tension builds as the judges compare tomatoes grown …" Click! "… wish you a Merry Christmas, we wish you …" Click! "Chartres Cathedral is one of the wonders of …" Click!

Opera! Click! Why was there nothing good on TV? Just a baby movie about singing cars he'd seen a million times already.

"I'm bored," moaned Henry. "And I'm starving."

He wandered into the kitchen, which looked like a hurricane had swept through.

"When's lunch? I thought we were eating at two. I'm starving."

"Soon," said Mum. She looked a little frazzled. "There's been a little problem with the oven."

"So when's lunch?" bellowed Horrid Henry.

"When it's ready!" bellowed Dad.

How long does Horrid Henry have to wait for his Christmas lunch? Find out in 'Horrid Henry's Christmas Lunch' from *Horrid Henry's Christmas Cracker*.

Christmas Crossword

Horrid Henry and his family are sitting down to Christmas dinner.
See if you can solve the picture clues and complete the crossword.

CLUES

DOWN

1. What colour is Pimply Paul's hat?

2. What type of meat are they having
for Christmas lunch?

3. How many are not wearing a hat?

ACROSS

3. How many are wearing glasses?

4. What colour is Mum's cardigan?

5. What does Dad's hat look like?
(Kings and queens wear one too!)

What We Like Best About Christmas . . .

PERFECT PETER

Best
Giving loads of presents to other people and seeing their faces light up with happiness.

Worst
Having to watch Henry's horrible TV programmes like Marvin the Maniac and Terminator Gladiator when he just wants to enjoy Manners with Maggie.

HORRID HENRY

Best
Getting loads of presents and eating as much chocolate as he can stuff in his mouth/steal off the tree.

Worst
Having to spend his hard-earned pocket money buying OTHER people presents when they should be thrilled to receive one of Henry's drawings or poems. When will other people learn it's the thought that counts?

DAD

Best
Doing lots of cooking and falling asleep in front of the telly.

Worst
Trying to stop Granny telling him how to peel sprouts, roast potatoes and make bread sauce.

MUM

Best
When Aunt Ruby, Stuck-Up Steve, Pimply Paul, Prissy Polly and Vomiting Vera leave.

Worst
Shouting at Henry all day, making sure Grandpa doesn't catch fire, cleaning up after Vomiting Vera.

STUCK-UP STEVE

Best
Getting more presents than anyone else.

Worst
Being related to Henry.

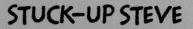

RICH AUNT RUBY

Best
Watching Steve spend all day unwrapping his presents.

Worst
Watching Steve brag about his presents and trying to stop him and Henry fighting.

MOODY MARGARET

Best
Having her parents do what she tells them all day.

Worst
Going back to school when Christmas is over.

GRANNY

Best
Telling her son that he is doing everything wrong, and not having to cook Christmas dinner.

Worst
Receiving a shower cap and a bumper pack of dusters as a present, when what she really wanted was a pair of red high heels.

MISS BATTLE-AXE

Best
Watching musicals on TV all day long.

Worst
Knowing Henry will still be in her class when school starts.

71

Pop-Up Creepy Christmas Card

YOU WILL NEED

3 pieces of A4 thin card
Pencil
Ruler
Scissors
Paints, crayons or felt-tip pens
Craft glue

INSTRUCTIONS

Diagram 1

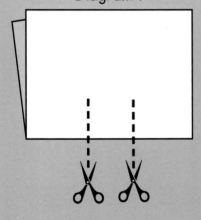

1. Fold two of the pieces of card in half. One half will be the outside of your card; one half will be the inside.

2. On the inside card, cut two parallel lines from the fold line to create your pop-up section (see Diagram 1).

Diagram 2

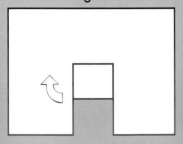

3. Fold over the flap that was formed by the cut and crease firmly (see Diagram 2).

Diagram 3

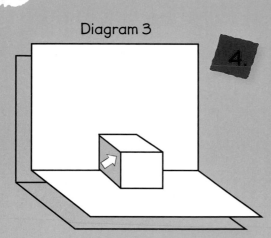

4. Unfold again, and open up your card. Push up the flap. Now you have a base to glue on a pop-up picture of your choice (see Diagram 3).

Diagram 4

5. Create your Christmas pop-up picture, and glue it to the pop-up section. When you open your card, your picture will pop up (see Diagram 4).

6. Decorate the outside piece of card, using paints, crayons or felt-tip pens, and glue it to the outside of the pop-up card.

You can draw whatever you like for your pop-up picture.
Maybe a Christmas tree or a snowman?
Or you can copy Horrid Henry's creepy-crawly spider!

Answers

Page 11

There are 11 cans of Fizzywizz on pages 20, 28, 31, 33, 42, 45, 47, 57, 58, 60 and 65.

Pages 20/21

1. YES – Henry orders snails by mistake at Restaurant Le Posh and loves them!
2. NO – It's called the Best Boys' Club.
3. NO – Perfect Peter won with his Snow Bunny.
4. YES – Perfect Peter got a star part.
5. YES!
6. NO – It's Moody Margaret who has the loudest scream ever.
7. NO – Lisping Lily wants to kiss and marry Horrid Henry.
8. YES – Bossy Bill was in big trouble!
9. YES – Horrid Henry won the election.
10. NO – Tidy Ted is one of Perfect Peter's best friends.

Page 22

1. 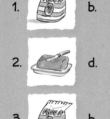 b.

2. d.

3. b.

4. c.

5. a.

Page 26

You can find the word FROGFACE 10 times.

The leftover letters spell out: **PONGY PANTS PIMPLE**

Pages 32/33

Page 37

The six differences are:
1. The 'P' is missing from Peter's suitcase
2. One of the stair posts is missing.
3. Peter's scarf is red instead of green.
4. Dad's trousers are green instead of brown.
5. Henry's shoe is white.
6. Mum isn't wearing her glasses.

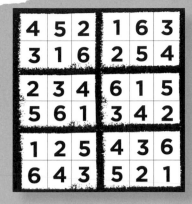

Page 40

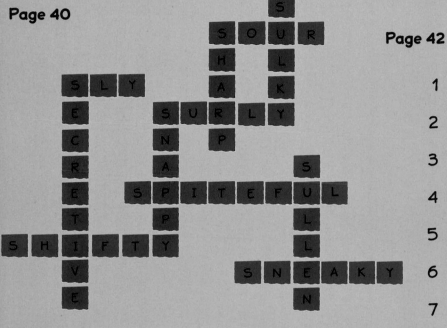

Page 42

1	S	A	T
2	N	N	H
3	E	D	E
4	A	G	M
5	K	R	N
6	I	A	O
7	N	B	W

SNEAK IN AND GRAB THEM NOW

Page 41

Page 46

1. C
2. V
3. WILLIAM
4. A / M
5. BERT
6. MARGARET
7.
8. S
9. RALPH
10.
11. G
BRIAN
13. LINDA
14. SUSAN
15. ANDREW

75

Answers

Page 53

Start and finish at Al's house

Pages 56/57

1. HIGH
2. DINNERS
3. RULER
4. HIVE
5. PUPILS
6. DRIVE
7. STICK
8. SMELL
9. MOAN

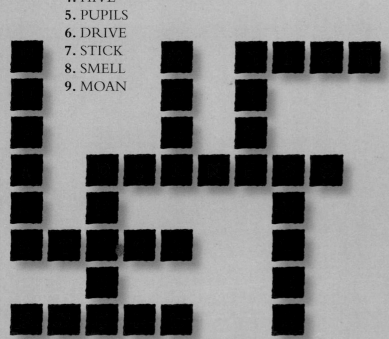

Pages 60-61

1. b
2. a
3. c
4. a
5. b
6. c
7. b
8. c
9. a
10. **a** = Beefy Bert
10. **b** = Rude Ralph
10. **c** = Clever Clare

Page 69

¹Y ²T

³T H R E E U

W L R

O ⁴B L A C K

O E

⁵C R O W N Y

You can read these other *Horrid Henry* titles, stories also available as audio editions, read by Miranda Richardson

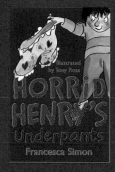

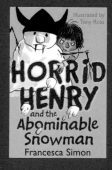
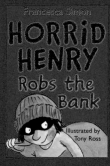

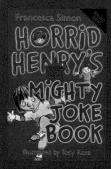